Jamarr R Stone

From Soldier To King

A Prisoner's Story of Pain, Regret and Redemption

Educated Thug Publications

Dedicated to:

Quinton "Q-Stone" Stone

The World Will Forever Be Your Stage

And To:

My Beautiful Baby Sister Jessye

Educated Thug Publications

Author's Note

If I described every event and individual I came in contact with over the course of my life this book would be a very voluminous body of work. My publisher asked for a specific amount of words and pages on this project and to adhere to the contract I had to narrow it down to the most notable events. So if you're not mentioned please don't take it personally.

I'd also like to stress that while life is built on perception, one person's sense of perception will undoubtedly differ from the next. This book is an interpretation of my life as I know it. This is my story *From Soldier To King*.

Educated Thug Publications

"People are always speculating—why am I as I am? To understand that of any persons, his whole life, from, birth, must be reviewed. All our experiences fuse into our personality. Everything that ever happened to us is an ingredient... I think that an objective reader may see how in the society to which I was exposed as a black youth here in America, for me to wind up in a prison was really just about inevitable."

Malcolm X

The Autobiography of Malcolm X 1965

Introduction

In 2004 I had an epiphany. That's the very first time I had a vision for this piece. And it didn't come subtle. It blossomed overnight like a rose from the concrete completely taking my mental and physical by storm. These thoughts couldn't stay bottled in. Somehow, someway I had to release them. But how?

In the beginning of 2004 I was detained and arraigned on one count of felony murder and sentenced to 15-years-to-Life in prison, and come summer I was already at my parent institution—Lebanon Correctional—where I'd spend the next five years shaping and molding my new identity. For those of you unaware Lebanon Correctional is hands down one of the worst prisons in the state of Ohio. From its pick of inmates and convicts to its deplorable conditions and its unyielding and relentlessly abusive and destructive staff, Lebanon is the bottom of the barrel. And this is where they sent me.

I wasn't intimidated by Lebanon's stature. After all I wasn't a choir boy myself. Growing up in one of Dayton, Ohio's most crime-laden neighborhoods, it was fairly easy adjusting to my new environment. And besides the fact that

I was either related to or associated with the main figureheads of this hellish institution, I'd managed to smuggle my street credibility through the barb-wired and gun-towered gates along with me. That said, I was well beyond safe. The only thing I had to worry about from that point on was how I'd do my time. Either I could allow myself to slip into the cusp of ignorance and stupidity by further perpetuating my life of crime and drugs, or I could begin the necessary healing process by manifesting change from the inside out. I chose the latter. And only for the fact that I was comfortable in my own skin and bore a strong spine was I able to pull this off. In environments like Lebanon being anything outside of their normal mold put a target on ones back. Thankfully, I was never a target.

As a twenty-two year old inmate of Lebanon I was definitely cut from a different cloth. I actually wanted better for myself and my children. I actually *wanted* to change, to be anything other than the childish, disrespectful and ignorant being that the street raised me to be. I had no idea that I'd be in the wildest and most spiritually draining journey of my life, but I'd already committed myself so it was what it was. From there on out I was destined to be a better man, to cherish life and strengthen and educate myself as much as possible, so that it was no longer ignorance and stupidity that I handed down to my children but instead strength, valor, morale, integrity, and discipline.

Outside of refraining from violence and drug use—and strengthening myself in terms of self-education and mastering my manhood—I had no way of leaving my imprint within the world. My folks weren't necessarily in my life full-stream at this time and what little family did involve themselves with me were so accustomed to my old ways that they pretty much just passed the "new me" off as a jail-house fad—as if I'd grown braids, massive muscles or got myself a brand new facial tattoo. They didn't know my actions were sincere and took every morsel of power vested in me by the Most High God to muster up. I didn't think—and still don't think—they believed I could change voluntarily. Not even if I wrote about it. Well, not if I wrote *them* about it.

It seemed as if nobody cared about my new positive lifestyle. I grew weary explaining myself, and it soon came to me that no matter how much I stressed my transformation that no one would believe me. I was Paul in the New Testament—a figurative Christian slayer—and the only way I'd be viewed in a different light was to do exactly what he done when he met Jesus: lead by way of actions and attributes not by tithe and tongue. But being crammed in a concrete box with two thousand identities is a recipe for destruction. And the fact that most are *Lifers* only made the situation worse. But there was something that I learned very quickly. As long as I didn't indulge in drugs, theft, gambling, sports (which I was never big on anyhow), or homosexual activities, I'd have a safe stay. All I had to do from there was dig down deep and discover who I really was and exactly what I wanted in life.

I've never been one to follow in the footsteps of others. In fact, I've been rebellious ever since I can remember. That said, being the follower-type who got wrapped up in other peoples mess was something I didn't have to worry about either. I had fourteen and a half years to cultivate a new me. But where did I start?

I've always been a storyteller. Whether joking or recanting my devious and impervious actions in the streets I could always hold an audience with captivating stories. I'd add a dash of color to certain stories to give my listeners that much needed laugh they were looking for, or stretch the truth in other areas to appease my crowd. It didn't take me long to realize I was on to something. Something big. Something that'd provide refuge from the streets. Something that would give me a sense of purpose in life and possibly provide an honest living outside of prison. I was going to be an author.

I hadn't read much at this point of my life. Although I liked reading and writing, I hadn't done much since taking my GED test in 2002. Outside of street signs, price tags, and restaurant menus I wasn't reading anything, much less writing. I had one helluva task ahead of me, but I knew I had to start somewhere. I picked up the Holy Bible and started a two-for-one. While strengthening my spirit and morale, I was also building my vocabulary and feeling around a good paragraph. You'd be surprised how much you can learn about writing from reading the Holy Bible. God works in mysterious ways…

By the end of 2004 I had the second vision for *From Soldier to King*. Little did I know but was soon to find out, God wasn't ready for me to share my story with the world. I hadn't stressed enough, grew enough, learned enough, and struggled enough. I needed more time to reflect, and while I bickered, griped and complained to God about my incompetence and inadequacy in terms of translating my thoughts, plans, wishes, feelings and aspirations, God said to me, *In due time, my son.... In due time.* And in due time it was.

What I didn't know then, but *fully* understand now, is that, while we have free reign in our lives to write and rewrite certain scenes, God is the Editor-and-Chief; He makes the final decision. And so, here I am, nearly eleven years and two appeals later, buckets of tears spilled and hundreds of hours studying my craft, and the Most High gives me the green light to put pen to paper. I know it won't be written perfectly from a literary stand-point, but it will be honest, authentic, inspirational and empowering.

With the weight of the entire world on his shoulders, he rose from the lowly rank of soldier to the regal rank of King, and he did so with valor, strength, honor, and integrity at heart...

God bless the child that can hold his own...

God bless the child that can hold his own...

PART: I

THE STREETS:
MY SURROGATE PARENT

<u>Chapter One</u>

Growing up was far from fair for me. I didn't have it as bad as a lot of the kids who grew up alongside of me, but the glass I drank from was far from half full. Being raised by a single black woman with a strong set of psychological and emotional issues of her own, I felt like my life was destined for pain and failure. Even at a young age I saw failure in my future. It seemed as if I were never good at anything besides crime and rebellion. I smoked cigars and weed at an early age and my fascination with guns kept me in juvenile hall or the probation department. And my mother tried. She'd chase me out and smack and punch me in the face and stomach, but her chastising never seemed to break me. I was a hardheaded little know-it-all who'd only learn by bumping his head.

Even though my mother was sometimes abusive, I knew she loved my brother Eric and me. We were three years apart and both Momma's Babies. A lot of people believe I was favored coming up but I believe the love she spread over us was equal. When one got the other got; if one suffered the other suffered too. But my mother was a beautiful spirit back then. Back before the spoils of the game ruined her. She was loyal to her family and community and her front door was always open. She'd clothe and feed practically anyone who needed it, and our three bedroom duplex on the West Side was always occupied by one of Gina's Angels. She'd console, nourish and feed them, and when she felt they were ready to fly off on their own she'd release them back into the wilderness of the streets.

Everybody knew about my mother, whether from her amazing acts of kindness or the wonderful drugs she sold. In a day where only brick-packed Mexican bud and Pine roamed the streets, anybody selling hydro was gonna stand out. And stand out she did. Everybody wanted a sack of Gina Momma's bud. Every major player and dealer in the city made their way to our Dayton View home to purchase a fifty dollar bag of the light green kind bud. They'd form lines outside or wait in their expensive vehicles until their turns came. They'd scored their bag, make a pass at my beautiful mother, or not, and quickly leave the residence to indulge themselves. And while my brother and cousin Billy (another of my mother's angels) watched by in wonder, I was busily being captivated by the allure of the game as well.

Speaking of The Game, it officially changed my life in 1993. I was twelve years old and my mother was knee-deep in the streets by now. Not only did she still sell weed, but she also started selling crack and coke as well. Now she didn't allow drugs to be consumed in the house, but I was still very intrigued by the life. My mother smoked weed and drank liquor (Remy Martin V.S.O.P.), but her drug of choice was prescription pills. Downers, always downers. Such as Xanax, Valiums and Somas. She'd take so many that she'd pass out and lose things, and I don't know why, but I wanted that. But not at first. In the beginning I despised my mother for popping pills. She wasn't the strong black leader I knew her to be when she was high. They made her normal, mediocre, another misled member of our miserable society. They made her the same as the prostitutes and dealers and addicts and pimps in our neighborhood. But how was it I wanted the same thing? How was it I wanted to be that high? I knew why she wanted it so bad, but what was I running from? My mother spoiled us. Every new video game or gym shoe we wanted we had. Every time I asked for something I received it. So why was I so desperate to be high? The answer was, I just wanted to be like her. But I never had the courage to take the pills from her. They were too few in volume and very much accounted for. But the weed she sold wasn't. And while I knew at that age it wasn't the same, weed would surely suffice. So I began stealing it. Everyday I'd dip my little yellow hand into one of the bulging Ziploc bags and steal between an eighth and a quarter ounce of the high-grade marijuana. I'd smoke it, sell it, and trade it in school for money and video games—and in no time my name spread. I gained status and notoriety throughout the neighborhood and school, but I also gained a bad marijuana habit. But who cared? At the end of the day all I wanted was to be cool. Who knew being cool would lead to life imprisonment?

My first issue surrounding marijuana occurred when my mother noticed her packages coming up short. And not just short short, but substantially short. Little did I know, but I was soon to find out, was that not only was I pilfering my mother's stash, but so was my brother Eric and cousin Billy. She came down hard on us, but I was damned if I was quitting. I had money in my pockets and I was popular, there was no way I was giving that up.

Everyone in my neighborhood was either selling crack or smoking it, so selling it for profit to purchase more weed wouldn't be a problem. I took fifty dollars, bought a gram and a half, and took to the streets. And it didn't take long before I was knee-deep in the streets. And I know I didn't need it. My mother worked and hustled on the side, and my father paid child support to support us. But I wanted to smoke weed and feel good and selling crack was the best way to do it. And it happened fast! I went from standing outside the local projects selling dimes in May to sitting in a wicker chair in the basement of an active crackhouse selling fifties in June. By thirteen I'd already lost my virginity to a crackhead, and driving hot or stolen cars was a pastime. I was moving at a very fast pace and absolutely fine with it. My mother was busy living a life of her own, brother and cousin chasing all the local teenagers, and my father was six blocks up on his second marriage with three step-kids and a wife to look after. No one noticed the change in me. No one besides the streets.

But I wasn't the only one undergoing a serious change. My mother—who'd pretty much lived her entire life opposite the law—was nearing a drawbridge of her own. Only problem was we were traveling in two different directions. After witnessing a close friend and neighbor lose his life to masked gunmen, and being a victim of armed robbery herself several months later, my mother decided to get out of the game while she still had the chance. She literally went cold turkey, not selling as much as a dime of crack or weed. Every customer was politely turned away, every shipment from her supplier gladly turned down. Mom's Duke had miraculously escaped The Game, only problem was, her youngest boy had just been caught in its snare…

*   *   *

By fifteen I managed to get in more trouble than the average adult in my neighborhood. Carrying a concealed weapon, fleeing and eluding the cops, and trespassing. I smoked weed constantly and drank hard liquor, and the pills, well they too were my drug of choice. Out of all the times I cried watching my mother incapacitated, all the prayers I sent up bartering my future for her sobriety, one would never expect me to follow the same path. But that's how addiction works. You seek what you see. And seek it I did! I'd pass out behind the wheel, fight people for no reason at all, and even destroy their property. I robbed, shot at people, and terrorized the streets. I can't count how many times I nearly lost my life in cop chases or gun-battles. I seemed to always be ruining somebody's life. I was a known hustler and shooter in the streets, but at home I was Mama's baby boy. I could do no wrong in her eyes, and to my father it was the same. Although he had a long-term drug addiction of his own, he still made an effort of consulting me. But I was programmed. The streets were all I wanted. So I'd shake my head and tell him I'd do better in the future, but as soon as his taillights were in the distance I was back smoking weed and popping pills and drinking; back selling crack and having sex with any crackhead or teenager that would open her legs for me. I had several relationships with girls my age and older and not once had I practiced safe sex or monogamy. I'd already been to the clinic for treatments of gonorrhea and crabs and it was an absolute blessing that that's all I caught. I was what the streets made me; I was pitiful.

By sixteen my life was utter disaster. Dayton Public Schools had already banned me from all campuses, and I was involved in so many crimes I couldn't keep track of them. Whether it was robbing rival hustlers or having all out shoot-outs with them I was always into something that involved death. I consumed more and more drugs and my rap sheet continued to get longer and longer by the year. I can honestly say that there was never another dull moment in my life after I started selling crack. More high-speed chases, trafficking drugs over interstate lines, and more gun battles. It got to a point where it wasn't safe for me to go out without a pistol, and I knew it was a definite possibility that I'd have to use it anywhere trouble arose: be it inside the mall or corner store, the doctor's office, even the local projects that sat adjacent to a police department.

Although it may not seem like it, I did have a heart. Just ask those closest to me. They knew the real me. The person who'd spend his last to help with rent or kids' school clothes. They knew that person. And I tried to keep the two entities separate. But try as I may, the other loomed closely around the corner…

By seventeen I was more of a hustler than the anything. But I'd been tied in to so many petty robberies and scandalous acts that a lot of major dealers were leery of me. But as I said, the people who knew me knew me. In the streets it's honor amongst thieves. So even though they knew it was a possibility that I'd turn, they kept me close. But if you were my guy you were my guy. I held pride in being loyal to those in my circle. There were guys I'd die for back then. They were my brothers, some of whom I spent more time with than my own family. And I loved my family. But the streets were more appealing and accepting. They didn't judge me. At home I was just Jamarr, in the streets I was a savvy hustler and gangster. I walked around with my pockets filled with money and pistols and felt appreciation. I saw people shot, killed, and sentenced to hundreds of years on the streets of Dayton, and somehow I felt a sense of pride. I laughed and smiled while roaming the streets like life was a joke. I had unprotected sex with young women and prostitutes as if the AIDS virus and other sexually transmitted diseases weren't running rampant, and continuously committed felony after felony as if I had immunity. I was young, wild, and reckless, and nothing would slow me down. Nothing except for fatherhood.

I missed out on my first child's birth. I caught her mother in the act of cheating and it hurt me to my core. It hurt so much that I abandoned her and denied our child. I even impregnated another woman. I hated my first child's mother for doing to me what I'd done to women since I started being with them, and I told myself that there was no way I was supporting a child that wasn't mine. That was my rationale. Forget the fact that I had unprotected sex with her and actually wanted the child. I'd caught her cheating and there was no way I was being anybody's sucker.

But the child was mine. And on September 20th, 1999, she changed my life. She was beautiful and undeniably mine. We named her Jamaria Charniece Stone, and the first time I looked into her little brown eyes I knew I'd been blessed. I was so happy to finally have something—someone—to actually call my own that I promised to live life differently. I knew I couldn't erase all the foul stuff I'd done over the years, but I was definitely gonna try. And, I knew I wasn't through with the streets, but I was pulling back. After all, I didn't have any skills outside of selling drugs—if you call that a skill. It was gonna be hard, but what in life isn't?

God wasn't through blessing me. On April 6, 2000, seven months after Jamaria was brought into this world, so was Jada Janae. I couldn't have been happier at that point! Now nineteen and head over heels in love with a woman named Andrea Carter, I felt life couldn't get any better. I had two healthy girls, a beautiful fiancée, and the street savviness of up and coming Hood Boss. By now I was taking my product on the road and distributing it small towns around the state of Ohio and the profit was welcoming. I decreased the work involved, increased the profit, and ultimately spent more time with my family. But my earlier teenage years continuously haunted me. I somehow still managed to find fights and engaged in violence, but it was all from my past and I hated it. I was much older and mature, and I wanted nothing but a life with my family. But that's how the streets are. Unforgiving, unforgiving, unforgiving. They don't care about your future, your life or your children. All they care for is your blood...

Chapter Two

From the years 2001-2002 I was incarcerated. For precisely eleven months Montgomery Education and Pre-Release Center was my home. The time resulted from a drug investigation in Springfield, Ohio, where thousands of grams of heroin and crack were allegedly sold by members of the Dayton View hustlers. I was charged with a laundry list of felonies—that ranged from possession of crack and tampering with evidence—on to felonious assault and firearm specifications. Most of the charges were trumped up and bogus, and the final result was the year I spent in prison. There were no halfway houses or drug Release Programs, I was meant to do the time. I thanked God, turned myself in to the proper authorities and was shipped off to my parent institution a few weeks later.

It was a piece of cake. There was virtually no violence—nor any tolerance for any—and acts of homosexual activity had never been recorded there. You were permitted through the compound as you pleased, and there was enough marijuana and tobacco to suffice a hippy. I was gonna fit in just fine.

My first week there I managed to secure a spot in solitary confinement. Charged with a Rule 19 fight and a Rule 39 under the influence I spent a month in isolation. My mouth ultimately got me into an altercation that my fist had to bail me out of. Just so happen, my eyes were bloodshot when the correctional officers detained me and a drug screen test was immediately ordered. I tested positive on the spot for marijuana and opium derivatives (Xanax) and given time in the hole. And it only got worse from there. In the beginning months at M.E.P.R.C. all I did was smoke weed. I occasionally did a push up or dip on the A-frames outside, but mainly I spent my time goofing off in Pre-GED class or on the phone with my fiancée Andrea. It was all play no work there. I had visits every week (with Andrea and my youngest daughter Jada) and dealt inwardly with my pain. I hated the fact that my fiancée was paying me back for my cheating ways, but I acted as if I didn't care. Other men were getting my love and it tore me apart inside. But what should I have expected? For it to feel good? If revenge was a dish best served cold this entrée was covered in icicles!

A couple months into my stay I was confronted by my teacher and threatened to be taken out of school. I was always rude and boisterous in class and a complete show-off for my homeboys. That was until the confrontation I had with my teacher. Suddenly I felt like a fool. There I was a man with adult responsibilities acting like a child. I straightened up forthrightfully and vowed to be done playing around in life. I quit smoking cold-turkey and hit the books overtime. I aced my Pre-GED and GED tests with flying colors, and quickly learned as long as I applied myself that I was capable of doing anything I put my mind to. And it was true. Here I was a guy who hadn't wrote or read anything in years and I passed both tests with flying colors! I was proud of myself, truly proud. But was I ready for a new life? Could I really straighten up and go square? I was a good man and father to some degree but could I stand firm underneath the overwhelming pressures of society? Would I be able to secure a job with numerous felony convictions and no experience, and if not how would I survive? I had three months to prepare myself—three months before I was back in the real world. This was gonna be a task, but I'd done everything else to bring forth change in my life. *Mise well start the process*, I told myself.

*   *   *

Before my timely departure from the Montgomery Education and Pre-Release Center I met a very striking and debonair individual named Pastor Carolina. My current cellmate suddenly moved out and in waltzed the pastor. He was brown-skinned, forty-plus in age and entirely incompatible to my standards. He was too quiet, minded his business entirely too much, and was overall a loner. Not my type of guy. Well, not at first. Then one day we started talking and suddenly Pastor Carolina became enjoyable. Mainly because he was from my birth place of Columbia, South Carolina, and up to this point I'd never met anyone besides my parents who'd been there. We left when I was three, and while I'd heard many good things about Columbia I couldn't remember a single thing to save my life. Then the Pastor moved in and within a week I was dyin' to go back. He had a beautiful family and massive home and promised to show me a good time if I visited. The pastor only had two months left on a Child Support

Charge (long story) and assured me that I wouldn't regret the decision if I decided to make the trip. I smiled and soaked it all up. Deep down inside I wanted to take him up on his offer but realistically I knew it would never happen. Dayton was my comfort zone; I couldn't fathom driving or flying hundreds of miles to merely see the sights. I had children, a fiancée, and very little cash to back the move.

So, I knew I'd never visit. But that didn't stop me from listening to the stories. And the more he told the more I saw myself in him. It was surreal to be honest. Turns out we were born in the same city, on the same day, and both hustlers at some point of our lives. We both loved our women and kids more than anything in this world, and both had relationships with God. *If ever I wanted to give up my life of crime and go straight*, I told myself, *now was the time.* And I did! Right there in front of Pastor Carolina I declared a decree to give up the life. I wanted better for myself and my children and I knew the streets only brought death and destruction. I had already lost one too many friends and family to the streets, I wasn't gonna be another casualty. I was out of the life.

The Pastor's sermons were what settled me. Now, I won't lie and say I was a full-fledged Bible thumper, but I was committed. I knew a few things now, and more than anything I knew what I wanted for my family. I decided that I'd use my newly acquired G.E.D. to enroll in college when I was released and that I'd humble myself to search for a nine-to-five to get me by. And I knew it was a long shot, but I loved my woman and children more than life itself. I couldn't risk leaving them again.

But two weeks prior to my release there was another change within me; one for the worst. I regressed. And during one of our midday conversations I expressed this to Pastor Carolina. I told him that I didn't have much to look forward to upon release and the streets were all I knew. But to be honest I was just afraid; afraid to embrace change, to reach out and touch something new. My decision would prove detrimental in the end.

My revelation brought tears to the Pastor's eyes. "Don't do this youngster," he said. "Please. There's more to life than streets. Trust me, I know... I used to be out there indulging, and look at all of what I've accomplished. I got land, a home, and a family. So what I'm locked up right now. I'm serving time for child support on a child that's been living with me for the past two years! And you know what? I don't mind being here. You know why? Because its guys like you who need me."

"I know, Pastor, but I ain't so fortunate," I said sadly.

"What you mean you ain't fortunate Jamarr? You have everything you need. You have health, family, God, and you have me. You wanna come live with me and my wife in South Carolina? C'mon now," he said with a huge smile on his face, "You always said you wanted to go back. C'mon, let's go call my wife... This way your fiancée can see it's real!"

I stood and followed the pastor to the phone room where I placed the call to my fiancée, who made a three-way call to his wife. As soon as she was connected I passed the receiver. "Hello, Baby?" the Pastor said. "Yes... I have Jamarr here, and he's faced with a serious problem... He feels he's gonna go back to the streets, and if he does we're gonna lose him. Um-hm... Yes. Yes... I'm sending him to live with us... Okay, well he gets out in two weeks, so please be expecting him. Yes, it's him and his fiancée.

Yup... We're gonna help 'em get situated. Yup, I'll help him get his C.D.L. license when I get there, and we'll get him a truck... Yes, yes... They can stay in the guest wing. Just make sure they're comfortable baby. Okay... See you soon!"

It went like that. And although the Pastor's offer was very rewarding and tempting, I couldn't accept it. I was a Ohio gangster who didn't know much outside of the streets I ran on. What would I do in South Carolina, who would I be? I wanted a life outside of the only one I knew but couldn't mooch off of the Pastor and his wife to get it. So I broke my vow right there before the Pastor. He dropped his head and cried. "You ain't gonna make it, Jamarr," he said between sobs. "Just give it a chance."

"It won't work," I said plainfaced.

"Just give it a shot, please."

"I can't... It won't work."

"You don't understand, Jamarr, you don't understand. You won't make it. I give you no more than 18 months before you're either dead or in jail for the rest of your life. Don't throw your life away like this Jamarr. Don't throw your life away."

And that was it. Nearly 18 months later to the day I was back in the Clark County Jail awaiting charges of murder, tampering with evidence and associated Firearm Specifications charges.

That was the first seasonal transition of my life. The second wasn't so much pleasant...

PART II:

MY JOURNEY INTO THE FIRE

Chapter Three

My homecoming from M.E.P.R.C. wasn't quite what I expected. Reason being, I had a completely twisted sense of reality when re-entering society. I thought I could sit back and silk life without actually putting forth any real effort. I had never had a tax-paying job, and I totally lacked any experience; I was too full of pride to work fast-food jobs or pay-a-day gigs, but I couldn't stand being broke either. Two-hundred dollars a week compared to a possible two thousand a day is a big transition. It was gonna be a difficult task. And then there was my past. My enemies weren't letting up and I'd been in so much BS over the years that even going to the local corner store unarmed was a risk. College was an option, and I tried. But after figuring the school checks wouldn't be enough to suffice the bills and babies I bailed out. I didn't last sixty days before I was back on Interstate 75 trafficking drugs. And it only took 48 hours; 48 hours later and I was $10,000 richer. I paid off my existing bills, moved to a more comfortable location and spent several thousands on my family's wardrobe. It was that easy. 48 hours. 48 hours and I went from being near broke and wanting more to having more and accepting less. The sad part was I was more foolish then ever. How so you ask? Because I knew better but chose worst. I chose to go against the grain and it would cost me more than I had to barter. Yes, I wanted away from the streets but I didn't want to struggle; I wanted to be a square and live a life free of crime but I wanted it with fast money and cars and easy women. But as we know I couldn't have them both. I was respected in the streets and knew how to get real money real fast and I wasn't ready to give that up. It was difficult. Picture being able to make tens of thousands of dollars at leisure, with little to no physical work involved, while having sex with beautiful women. It sounds easy to give it all up in an instant but it's actually one of the hardest things in life for us hustlers to do. The streets deceive us to the point of delirium. We see clear the positives but the negatives hide from us in plain sight. We see how the streets make us men and providers for our families but refuse to see how it makes us cowards in the eyes of the world. Take me for example: I became mentally and physically abusive to my fiancée, drank and ate Xanax daily as if that would supplement my inadequacies, lashed out at her several times a month—as if it were her fault that I wasn't a real man—and like the strong black woman she was she took it with a grain of salt and worked towards maintaining her family. Ms. Andrea S. Carter will forever be one of the strongest and beautiful people I know. She endured the cheating, the abuse, and she still loved me through the midst of it all. Hell, if you ask me she was the real man of the relationship.

*   *   *

One of the best things that happened in those eighteen months of freedom after M.E.P.R.C. was we got pregnant. Neither of us had been happier. And the fact that our child was never supposed to survive birth due to a high-risk pregnancy meant all the more. He was a blessing, a miracle. We planned him and he came. And I slowed down some, but the streets only allow so much. I saw the vision of a better life, but it wasn't until I caught another gun charge that the vision became crystal clear.

*   *   *

My son's mother was 6 months pregnant and more beautiful than I'd ever seen her; her cheeks were sweet and puffy, eyes bright and clear, skin smooth and flawlessly radiant. I on the other hand looked like shit (excuse my language). The streets had worn me down. My eyes sunk into the hollow sockets of my face and my heart was heavy as steel. Dark worry lines creased my forehead and crow's feet were starting to form underneath. I'd just been robbed by a close friend for nearly twenty thousand dollars in cash and drugs, gotten into two shoot-outs, and had a thirty-thousand dollar bounty on my head for the mischievous deeds of my past. I was hollow inside and the only thing that was keeping me focused was the birth of my son. I bought him clothes and things daily and kept pictures of his soon-to-be first steps in my mind. I pictured his first smile and basketball game and what it would be like to show him how to tie his shoes and fish. I thought of all the fatherly stuff I'd do with him and how we'd be inseparable throughout everything, but even then the streets were still close by. There was an incident where I was sitting in my car outside of a local corner store when the cops swarmed me. A guy from an early altercation had seen me pull up and called the cops. I was snatched out, caught red-handed with a pistol and crack and cash and not only booked on those charges but charges that alleged I'd shot at him a few months back. I kept my mouth shut, contacted my attorney and immediately started sending up more prayers. I needed to be present for my son's birth. My fiancée needed me, he needed me, and a larger part of myself needed to be there. But, the question was: would I make it?

<u>Chapter Four</u>

It was 18th months after being released from M.E.P.R.C. and my life was starting to settle. Everything I prayed for had come to fruition. I successfully made it off parole, and the corner store case was nearly over. The only thing I was waiting on was a call from my attorney to determine if I'd get probation for the carrying a concealed weapon charge or not. I'd already dropped clean urine for preliminary probation screening and everything was looking good. Until my fiancée and I had a conversation one evening and she posed the question: *Would you give it all up if God granted you one last wish?* Of course, I told her. I wanted nothing more than to live my life with my wife and my children. Never mind the fact that I only had about fifteen thousand to my name and no plan B or C to fall back on. To be honest, I just didn't wanna do more time. It was a good chance that I'd lose my fiancée if I did, and if that happened I'd die inside. She was the only thing outside of my children that I had positive in the world. She was my friend, my confidant, my love, my rock. She was my everything. And I did have family, but family rarely loves you when you really need to be loved. Either they don't know you or don't take the time to discover you. Andrea did. With her I could be myself. She knew me better than anybody. More than my mother, brothers, sisters or father. She taught me everything I knew about my girls and blessed me with a beautiful baby boy. I couldn't lose her. I just couldn't. And two weeks after the question and vow to the Most High God I received the call from my attorney. "Mr. Stone," he said to me, "I have good news! The judge approved your probation today!" I was beaming. "We have a court date scheduled in one week from today where we'll finalize it!" I was ecstatic but managed to hold it in. My fiancée and I were in the car headed for the mall and although she knew who I was talking to she didn't know about what.

So I thanked the attorney and very calmly turned to my fiancée. "What?" she asked smiling. "What did he say?"

I paused for a second for drama then I yelled, "Probation! Probation! He got me probation!" She was happy, genuinely happy. Out of all the bullshit I'd taken her through in life she was happy for me. But deep down inside

I was the same old morally ill person. I looked to Andrea, and right then broke my vow. "I need you to get me a rental car," I said plainfaced and placid.

"For what?" she asked through a pair of knitted eyebrows.

"So I can hit Detroit, I'm expanding."

"Expanding?" Andrea asked as her eyes filled with tears. "But I thought you were done?"

"You think fifteen thousand gone support us? How long you think that shit gone last? What, you gone support us?!"

I flipped out and became naturally defensive because I was caught. I wasn't worried about my commitments to her or God for that matter and it showed. I had achieved my goal and eluded prison and that's all that mattered to me at that point. I was insane, afraid, and selfish. And six days later the Pastor's prophecy about me came true.

February 26th 2004 the indictment of Murder and Tampering With Evidence with a Firearm Specification came down. I was crushed! I couldn't eat or sleep and the wheels of my mind wouldn't stop turning. So many things were running through my head that I had temple pulsating migraines. Like all the foul stuff I'd done, all the negativity and illicit deeds were running through my mind at once; all the times I put my life and the lives of those who loved me in jeopardy; all the shortcuts I took in life, all the drug sales and high-speed chases; all the lies, the broken hearts and abuse. In a way I felt like I deserved to be incarcerated. Not for murder, but for all the crimes I committed and gotten away with in the past. And that's how karma is. When she returns she returns with vengeance. Here I was the victim of a vicious attack, in a crowded nightclub, buy a violent, drunken individual and the prosecutor pegged me as the aggressor! I'd never been so humble or worried in my life than I was that night but I was the problem? I'd never been spoken to in the manner I was spoken, threatened to such a degree or physically assaulted so badly in my life, but I was the problem? I only wanted to have a good time and protect my brother who was present that night, but I guess it was my destiny that I suffered in the manner I did. I'd never been so spiritually drained, so morally corrupted, and somehow I strangely felt that I deserved it. I let my family down, my community, and more than anything God. I hurt people, worshipped graven images and made endless empty promises. Now was time for payback. I ended up with Fifteen-Years-To-Life. They illegally threatened witnesses, withheld exculpatory evidence and the result was I admitted to a charge I didn't commit for a possibility of freedom some day. The way I saw it was this: Fifteen and fifty years are a big difference. And while I was technically innocent of the charge in which they held me on, it was the right thing to do. It was time that I started taking accountability for my actions, and what better way than by providing closure for the deceased family? I pled guilty and thirty days later was arriving in Lebanon Correctional.

*　　　*　　　*

My first thought of Lebanon was: This is real prison! It was wild and crazy everyday and the gang fights and assaults were brutal. The food was horrible, the water contaminated and the rats and roaches out-numbered the inmates a thousand-to-one. There were no washing machines or dryers, you showered next to two naked men and no man was exempt from beatings by the guards. Quite frankly, Lebanon was a hellhole. And it only did one or two things to its inhabitants. Either it made them extremely better or extremely worse. Either way, it made you.

For me Lebanon was a blessing. I forced out all the drugs and intoxicants from my life and worked steadfastly at discovering who I really was as an individual. And within a year I was made different. I was better, stronger, and most certainly more proud of myself. I won't lie and say the journey wasn't painful or sometimes overwhelming, because it was. But it was very much needed and this was the beginning of my transformation from soldier to king.

No one seemed to recognize the true change within me though. Well, not the people who I owed my transformation to; people like my children, parents, and more importantly my son's mother. She witnessed me at my lowest of lows and probably didn't think I was capable of change. I tried my best to convince her different but she only gave up on me. She was my everything, my all, and she left me when I needed her most. But I understood why. She was sick and tired of being sick and tired and it was time that she escaped. Only problem was I was sure my time in prison would be dramatically different now. I didn't deal with my other children's mothers and I'd cut ties with every other female from my past out of respect for her. I decided that I wouldn't continue cheating so I let them go. But now she was gone and I had to accept all the pain that came with it. And I knew she was gonna leave one day, I just didn't expect it to be so soon. She lasted literally three years to the day of incarceration, and although I still wanted her in my life as my wife, I had to let her fly off in peace. She'd done everything in her power to bring ultimate comfort to my life, there was no way I could keep her caged in. I pushed her out of my mind and heart and immediately moved on...

I took the split pretty bad. The distance between us seemed like light years away, and if not for my two friends Shawn Lillard and Ebony Porter I can't say where I'd be now. They played truly monumental roles in my journey. Shawn stood in the wilderness with me while I hand-battled the elements and Ebony provided the much needed mental and emotional support that I needed to survive. She became my heart and soul outside of prison and he was my shrink inside.

With Ebony the new twinkle in my eye I was able to think and breathe differently. Her vibrant smile and outgoing nature was therapeutic. I was drunk in love and somehow well over my son's mother. My stomach no longer tightened when I thought of her with another man and I never got jealous when I heard things. We managed to maintain a plutonic relationship for the sake of the kids and I was okay with that.

And Ebony did more than simply appeal to my manly senses. Although she was attractive and respected and loved me, she motivated me to think and grow beyond my environment. She sent books and urged that I read more. She challenged me with thought-provoking questions and demanded that I answered them truthfully and forthrightly. We'd vibe back and forth about novels and certain characters in those novels and always she'd say, "You been through so much... Why don't you write a book?" I put it off so many times but she'd always come back to it. "Why don't you do it? You're smart enough, and you can write, so do it." I finally took her advice and put pen to paper one day. I wrote and wrote and finally finished the rough draft to my first novel. Only thing was, she left before it was ever published. I was heartbroken all over again, but like the old saying goes: *When one door closes, another one opens...*

*   *   *

Nearly five years had passed and I still hadn't had any real communication with my brother Eric. The last time I'd seen him was the night of the incident at the nightclub, and although we'd spoken a few times, neither of us were tearin' at the walls of silence to further our bond. The entire collect call system was more difficult back then, and at this time my brother was on probation for felony theft. He had a new wife and complicated issues surrounding visitation rights with his ex so life was already stressful enough. But this was my big brother. I had a younger biological brother and one other step-brother but Eric was my second heartbeat. He fed and cared for me when I was younger and was always my idol. *How could he turn his back on me at a time like this?* I'd ask myself. And so many questions crossed my mind, but the only way to find out was to get him down and ask him myself.

I sent Eric a visitation form to complete and he was approved under special circumstances the next week. He made the 15 minute drive south, braved the vigorous screening process and was subsequently admitted inside the facility to visit me.

I entered the visitation room that day a ball of emotions. On one hand I was extremely gratified to see him but on the other end I was pissed that he'd waited so long to come. So over bland vending machine food and cold sodas we worked at tearing down the walls of silence that separated us. We talked about family, how my niece (his daughter) was doing, how my kids were doing, even our grandparents. We talked, talked, and talked and I still hadn't touched the subject of abandonment. But I couldn't hold out any longer. "I wanna know why I haven't heard from you?" I suddenly blurted out, and the conversation quickly went from casual to serious.

"I ain't never did this jail shit bro," he said starting to cry. "I know I ain't been there for you and I'm sorry. All this stuff new to me, but if you give me a chance I'll make it up to you bro…"

I placed my hand on his shoulder. "It's cool, bro..." I said to him. "Just promise me you'll never leave me again; promise me that."

He looked me clear in the eyes and promised. "I'll never leave you again I promise. We all we got..."

And like that I got my brother back. We finished eating and 2008 ended on a rather good note. I lost two women in four years but gained my brother. I was definitely blessed!

<u>Chapter Five</u>

2009 started on a beautiful note. Word traveled around compound that tobacco was undergoing a ban statewide. At first I couldn't believe it, wouldn't believe it. But when the staff began griping about it I knew it was true. This meant they couldn't chew dip or smoke tobacco on the premises and they were pissed! Seeing how most of them were rednecks who grew up smoking and drinking this sudden revelation was like pulling teeth! But that wasn't the only change. Prices for contraband tobacco were gonna sky-rocket in the next few months. Banning one of the most sought-out substances since the inception of incarceration could be a major issue. Not only would it cause a high influx in cash for inmates and staff alike, but it would also open up doors for prisoners like myself who were trying to gather the necessary funds to hire an attorney. I'd filed numerous Pro Se appeals (using my own wit and know-how) but at that point none of them sufficed. Therefore, selling tobacco was probably going to be my only shot at making an appeal. So I prayed and prayed and prayed and through the power of my sub-conscious mind received an answer. *Go. Stock up...* It said. *Sell everything... Tap into every resource you have... The beginning to your Expected End is near...* And I did just that. I sold everything I had inside the prison (c.d.'s, rare shoes and clothes, even my extensive porn collection) and stocked up while tobacco was still legal. From there I waited...

At this point of my prison stay I hadn't done much of anything illegal. I smoked weed a handful of times and dropped off a few packages for a homeboy but other than that I was a square by prison standards. As I said before: I didn't indulge in gambling, stealing, or homosexual activities, so selling contraband tobacco was the first serious infraction I committed. I'm just glad everyone around me didn't have the same proverbial lightbulb to appear over their heads.

When the ban first-surfaced I would've missed out had I not listened to my sub-conscious. I sold the tobacco and stocked up before it was actually an infringement of DRC policy and managed to retain the counsel of my choice. My status was decreased to medium for good behavior and my security transfer to another institution was pending. I managed to stay trouble-free for five years to qualify for the transfer but now that I was actually eligible to leave I didn't really want to. Why? Because to leave meant I was leaving behind one of my best friends in a long time. To leave meant I was leaving behind Tweet.

Raham "Tweet" Twitty had become my brother over the course of the five years I'd known him. From day one he and I were close. He was infectious, humble, and generous, and while most saw a convict and cop-killer in him I saw a beautiful soul who made a fatal mistake; I saw a victim of circumstance, a reason why not to mix anger with drugs. That's what I saw when I looked at Tweet. He was kind, sympathetic, and lovable, but he made a mistake—a mistake that cost him a life of pain, degradation, and ultimately death. He ate a handful of prescription Xanax and made a poor decision that involved his fiancée. They had a verbal dispute outside their home and the cops were called. When they showed up Tweet foolishly drew an assault rifle and demanded them off his property. He didn't truly mean any harm. He was high, upset, and out of his own mouth, "seeking attention" from his fiancée. But the cops didn't see it that way. They saw the weapon in his hand and followed protocol. They let off the first round of shots and freakishly one of their bullets struck Tweet's right hand. His finger hit the trigger, and in turn the one bullet that exited his gun that fateful day struck Officer Mary Beal in the neck paralyzing her on impact. Tweet was shot in his chest, arms, legs and feet that day, and ultimately sentenced to 76 years in prison. Mary Beal died several years later due to alleged complications with her paralysis, and Tweet passed 10 years later in Lebanon Correctional Institution due to a brain aneurysm.

I remember many, many things about Tweet, but the main things that stick out are his energetic smile and unbreakable peace within. I never seen him angry, and only once had I witnessed him sad. It was the week before I transferred from Lebanon to London and we were in the prison library saying our departures. Tweet had been moved to the Super Merit block on the opposite wing of the prison for exceptional behavior so contact was limited. Our only medium was the prison library, so we scheduled a day and finagled our way down the hallway at the specific time. We dapped, hugged and took up a seat near the back of the library where we quickly caught up on family, friends, and life outside of prison. The visit ended bittersweet for Tweet. He was happy that I'd made it out of hell but sad that I was leaving him behind. But I was too. This was my brother, a person whose presence I appreciated in life just as much as I did Eric, and I was leaving him behind till God knew when. It was a somber day for me, but even more somber for Tweet. With tears in his eyes he looked across the table at me and mumbled: "Come back and get me bruh... Don't let me die in here... You're my only shot. Come back and get me..." He put his bullet-riddled hand on mine and cried unabashedly. That was the last time I saw him. He passed a year later while I was in London Correctional. His memory will forever live on...

*　　　*　　　*

London was a serious transition for me. Coming from a secure cell block atmosphere to a open dormitory was definitely a difficult change to endure. I was used to being in Lebanon where the threat level was always high and violence imminent; where seasoned convicts roamed the land with fistfuls of hope and hearts full of malice. Hell, my first couple days there I saw guys bricked, stabbed in the face and stomped within inches of their lives. Now I was in London and I half expected it to be crazy. I'd heard so much talk about medium security institutions with their short-timers and openness that I anticipated the worst. Especially given the fact the prison was located fifteen minutes away from where I caught my case. I pictured twenty or thirty locals waiting for me when I stepped off the bus and having to fight them all. And I'd been in so many foolish situations in my past that I couldn't blame them. Although I was a different person inside I couldn't turn back the hands of time. It was time that I face this new chapter of my life like I'd faced all the others in the past: with optimism but without fear.

My first impression of London was *this is a joke!* Guys ran up and down the aisles laughing and yelling and disrupting the C.O.'s during their mandatory counts. It was a playpen, not a prison. The movement was non-stop and every inmate was a potential problem. As said, I was accustomed to locked doors and sleeping in partial peace, not amongst two hundred hark-ankles in the open. But this was my new residence so I had to press forward and make the best of it.

My chances of obtaining a college education at that time was out of the question. Per DRC policy I had too much time left on my sentence. They required inmates to be within five years or less to qualify for any college courses. But I picked up a craft while at Lebanon, one that would serve as a beneficial tool towards success while I was there at London. I worked as an Advanced Data Entry Clerk (for the Ohio Penal Industries) and completely learned my way around a computer. I was keying upwards of 70 words per minute, and when added to my love and a knack for writing I was sure something would spring up. And it did! The Writer's Workshop London, Ohio branch. The program was sponsored by Urbana College and offered insurmountable benefits to aspiring writers. There I could write, read, and most importantly gain access to the colleges computers. It was a wonderful program if you managed to get accepted. The only problem was you had to be a member of the college to actually do so, and seeing how I was ineligible I was out of luck. Or so I thought. After submitting a chapter of my work to the professor and program foreman I was accepted under special circumstances. Things were getting better for me in prison. Now, if only I could move past the abandonment issues…

Chapter Six

It is not possible for a man exposed to several degrees of abuse, isolation, and depravation not to develop depression born out of extreme rage repressed over a long period of time. It is simply a question of when and how the depressive reaction will surface and manifest itself.

Lorde Dominic Pressler III

This statement is stunningly true. And it's universal; for guys like myself—guys seeking spiritual and mental enlightenment—as well as knuckle-head ruffians. Everybody needs somebody in life. Even the most heartless and ruthless convicts need a caring hand to caress their rugged exteriors. That's just the way it is. And abandonment is probably the most critical element within incarceration. Well, that and the fear of dying. But it's not just the thought of dying, because to die is to die. Who cares how you die? But to die unfulfilled is a totally different dimension of that fear. Prison stagnates you so much that you feel defeated; defeated from not having properly educated your children or traveled the world, or even having made amends to those you've wronged in life. You miss out on birthdays and holidays and special moments and when you mix those with abandonment you have a Molotov cocktail of rage and depression. When the love your family and friends have for you fades you slowly fade into the fabric of your environment and you begin to feel worthless. The degrading process with visiting and collect calls gets old to 'em and they become accustomed to your absence. That's when the lack of communication becomes normal and you feel as if you're imposing on their lives. So you place even more distance between you and them, that's when the days turn months, months turn into years, and the years turned into decades. The seasons change with the wind, and, if you're on top of your game you change right with them. For the better that is. For me, my abandonment issues manifested into fruit. And I'm not fully free of them—and it is still painful at times—but like most things painful, if it doesn't actually kill you it only makes you stronger.

The beauty within my struggle is that it forced me to take writing more seriously. When I grew lonely I wrote and read. When a visitor didn't show or I missed my kids to the point where I couldn't stop crying, I wrote or read. I became the characters and the characters became me. I took pleasure in living their lives and loved learning new techniques and styles. I began reading books on format, style and editing, and introduced every thing of what I learned to the Writer's Workshop. But the problem was I would never be totally fulfilled. At least not by writing alone. So I turned to drugs.

As said, I only smoked weed maybe five or six times while at Lebanon. Twice when I first got there and three or four times before I was shipped out five years later. The first two times I freaked out thinking how the last of my days were gonna be spent in a cage, and the others were to treat my unsettling anxiety. My up and coming transfer was digging at me something serious. I didn't know what to expect and my past wasn't so welcoming. Prescription meds were out the question. My pride wouldn't allow me to be placed on a psychiatric caseload. Especially a drug I knew nothing about. So, I foolishly reached out and located marijuana to stimulate my mind and calm my nerves. That was one of the biggest mistakes I made in a long time.

No matter what people say, tobacco and marijuana are gateway drugs inside prison. Meaning, every other ill-gotten activity or substance can be met through these two. Narcotics, stolen goods, even alcohol or weapons. I never dealt drugs at that point and damned sure wasn't a thief or focused on locating weapons. I was a proverbial square, a converted gangster. Then came the tobacco and the weed, and before I knew it I was poking my head down into the bowels of London's evil underworld. I went through a stage in my life where I was hell-bent on proving my innocence to the charge of murder, and I felt as if the word of God was directing me towards the illegal activity. The passage in James 2:17 in the Holy Bible about faith without works struck a cord. To me it translated that no matter how much faith I had that without putting in the necessary work to fund paralegals and attorneys that I would never achieve my goals. I missed my kids dearly, and had a burning flame inside me to make it out before 2019 to break the generational curse on them. The few people I had in my corner were living check to check and I felt the best way to achieve the goal was to hustle. Another foolish mistake.

I was always loving and caring towards my kids. Even from a jail cell. But with more money the love increased. So instead of sending letters and pictures it was plush teddy bears, balloons, or money for wardrobes. If a new game or doll came out and they wanted it all they had to do was ask and a week later it was at their doorstep. Of course I could've done more if I was free, but I was making the best of my situation. It drew me closer to my children and their mothers were happy to have a helping hand. I guess you can say hustling had its rewards.

I took a long break from smoking weed and focused steadfastly on writing, studying and fighting my case on appeal. The gaps of abandonment were being filled with every thousand I made and I ultimately grew closer with self. I was learning and evolving and quite naturally I felt better. If only it would stay that way. Then I fell back from weed altogether. I wasn't up for all the unnecessary heat that came with it. It was too bulky and too problematic to deal with. I never wanted to be the man in prison. I wanted to amass revenue and continue paying my attorney's fees and possibly self-publish my first novel. I wasn't up for getting jammed and piling burning coals on my head before the parole board. And, to be honest, I didn't want to hustle anymore. It's so much more peaceful not involving yourself in drugs and infractions while incarcerated. Never knowing when you'd be drug tested or served a random search is terribly stressful. But so is the thought of dying an unaccomplished man in prison. I know it was good to have faith, but even the Good Book says, "Faith without works is useless." And so, I made myself 'useful'. I regret the decision now, but like always, at that point it couldn't have been a better course of action for me.

So, heroin became my thing. It was small, odorless and very high in profit. With a few simple sales I could handle my business, make the money count, and all would be well. But it's never that picture perfect easy.

I was sitting in my cell in the Merit Block (ironically a place where you're housed for good behavior) and the thought crossed my mind of what it'd feel like to indulge in the White Horse. And I'd never had this itch. Never. I'd spent weeks in roach and rat infested shooting galleries, junkies polluting their bodies with heroin and cocaine mixes, and never had I the urge to use. But I'd never been so emotionally alone like I was either. I had visits quite often and bothered people on the phone daily, but I was still empty inside. Out there I had women and friends and other drugs to rely on to coax the pain. I guess you can say drugs that were more socially acceptable. I had weed, liquor, and Xanax (which was said to compare to heroin). But I didn't have that now. All I had was heroin. So, I broke down one of the capsules and took a whiff. Then another. I then cleaned up behind myself and got dressed while I waited for my name to be called over the loudspeaker for visitation. A childhood associate and his girlfriend were scheduled to see me within the hour and I was looking forward to the meeting. And I know what you're probably thinking. What about the deadly narcotic in my system, huh? Well, for some reason I didn't feel it. Either I'd sniffed it wrong or not enough. So after my visit I took to my stash and took out another bag. I snorted the entire dose in one whiff. How silly of me. Within ten minutes my entire body was flushed and my stomach twisted in knots. My nose burned like 151 proof rum and a prickly feeling replaced my feet. This was The Rush the junkies coveted—the rush they chased to their graves. I felt like heaven but looked like hell, and for just that moment I didn't have a care in the world. With the icy December snow underneath my feet, and dozens of unidentical snowflakes on my face, I looked up at the sky and said aloud: "You can take me right now. My family doesn't give a fuck about me, my kids are growing older without me, and I'm serving a life sentence for a charge I didn't commit." I rubbed my nose as the mediciny fluid drained from my nasal passage down into my esophagus and swallowed just as my homey Joe walked out of Cell Block C.

Joe and I made the ride from Lebanon to London together and remained close ever since. He was ten years in on a twenty year murder/robbery deal and like Tweet had a genuine soul. "What up bruh?" Joe asked looking at the boots I wore specifically for visits. "I see you all fresh. Who came down?"

"Nell and Nikki," I responded without giving him much eye contact.

"Must've been nice. See you out here in December in a V-neck and Tim's," he said smiling.

"Yeah… I just came out to get some air."

"Oh. You takin' the walk wit' me?" he asked referring to the cafeteria for dinner.

"Yeah… C'mon, I'm wit' you…"

Joe and I made the three or four minute trek to the cafeteria and I sat down beside him and offered my tray. He gladly accepted and scooped the Main off. Meanwhile, I was slipping into an intense state of nirvana. My body heated up even more and my brain twirled in my head; my heartbeat slowed down and the food from visitation sloshed around in my stomach like water in a fish bowl. And just before I threw up, Joe spoke: "You cool, bruh? You look sick." I blinked my eyes and wiped my face. "Yeah… I'm good. I ate… I ate some swine out there." Then suddenly: "I'm outta here bruh!" I quickly gave Joe dap and dumped the remainder of my tray in the garbage can on my way out the door, and just as the cold winter air whipped against my flushed cheeks I said aloud, "Never again… Never again…"

<u>Chapter Seven</u>

2010 and 2011 seemed to merge themselves together as one. I continued to elevate my mental capabilities by learning self and perfecting my craft and things picked up for me. I had more visits from family and friends and my resources multiplied beyond measure. My fellow writers looked forward to my presence at our weekly meetings as well did my six man workout crew. All was well… Well, until jealousy found its way into my cipher.

The only rule infraction I had since leaving Lebanon in August of 2009 was a tattoo ticket. I served roughly three weeks in Segregation and 90 days on sanctions (meaning no visits, commissary or television privileges) for the infraction. I also lost my bed in the merit block and got bumped back down to a normal dormitory living arrangement. The risk definitely wasn't worth the rewards. As much as I like ink, the infraction was foolish. But I had time to reflect on my decisions while in Segregation. I also had time to dissect my first manuscript. At this point I had donated *years* to perfecting my craft and I wondered when my first flower would spring forth. Little did I know, a physical altercation in which I'd have to defend would come first.

The situation occurred not long after I was moved out of the Sanction Block and back to a regular dorm. By random placement I was paired up with a guy to whom a close friend of mine strongly disliked. The issue was, my partner Fred (who was free at the time), started having relations with this guy's woman, and the guy—my new bunky—found out and started bad mouthing him to people on the streets. Now it wasn't really an issue because Fred was free and able to deal with the woman in question, but men are territorial creatures and my partner was upset. So was my new bunky, but he didn't show it. We had a brief conversation about my close relationship with Fred— including my undying loyalty to him—and after it was clear that there'd be no more bad mouthing him I unpacked my things and settled in.

The most complicated thing about my new bunky was the fact that he was very close to a guy that I'd grown close to named ATL. ATL was a cool lightskin guy from Atlanta who'd recently given the state of Ohio 28 years back on a 34 year drug sentence by way of appeal. He was calm and laid back but a renegade by prison standards. He smoked weed every single day like it was legal, and made lots of money in the institution while doing so. He had sex on the visit as if the state of Ohio condoned in congugals, took good care of his daughter from inside, and demanded respect from the correctional officers and inmates. He was a damned good guy and he quickly grew on me. But so did his partner (my new bunky), and before I knew it the three of us were inseparable. I finally published my first novel (Trapstarz, with Author House Publications) and finished paying off my attorney fees and my guys were genuinely happy for me. Or so I thought. Our clique was all daps and smiles, until something changed in my bunky.

For those of you unaware of the mechanics of prison absolute silence from a bunky or cellmate can be very serious. All types of things can plague the mind of a prisoner, and although you really wanna ask what's going on, you truthfully don't wanna know. I've seen countless guys lose their wives, children, and parents in prison, and the aftermath that follows. I've seen guys melt their bedmate's faces off, stab them, even kill them in their sleep for things as trivial as waking up to use the restroom too

many times at night. I was definitely worried so I gave him
his space and paid real close attention to his actions. But
come to find out, my bunky's problem was with me! Yes,
apparently he'd grown tired of dealing with the guy whose
best friend was dealing with his woman and he couldn't
take it anymore. While others were around he'd smile and
chuckle but in their absence he was always mute. I
shrugged it off and told myself everything was cool. Two
days later he attacked me. We were both in the gymnasium
working out and he flipped out. I later found out that he'd
been on the phone talking to a family member when my
partner and his girl walked in the room. In an instant all our
months of building and breaking bread was thrown out the
window. I'm no longer an advocate for violence so I won't
get too in depth on what happened that day. However, I
will say it didn't end well for him. No only did he lose his
girl but he lost the fight as well. The only thing was, I lost
too…

*   *   *

Mid 2011 my attorney contacted me and advised that our Motion to Vacate and Set Aside sentence was denied, and that if I intended to appeal I needed to start scraping up the necessary funds to do so immediately. I was hurt and at a loss for words. They denied me from my admission of guilt saying that since I agreed to the charge in question that my sentence of fifteen-years-to-life should stand. Never mind the fact that I accompanied the motion with seven sworn affidavits from eye-witnesses attesting to the fact that not only did I try to avoid the entire situation that night, but that I was threatened, assaulted, and ultimately pursued out of the club by a very violent and aggressive individual. I supplemented the motion with original hospital records and photos that depicted my injuries, even documentation that proved that my attacker had a silver cellular phone in his hand when he was shot— one that he used to portray the image of a weapon. I also illustrated my trial attorney's obvious incompetence during the pre-trial aspect of my case, and showed with clear and convincing evidence that my constitutional rights were violated. But, I had given up my rights when I pled guilty said the judge. Now I was destroyed, broke, and although I hated having to resort back to hustling to get the job done I felt like I didn't have any other choice. With only a thirty day window before the motion would sink, I owed it to myself and children to come up with the money. I made the biggest mistake of my life by not getting out the game when the Pastor told me to and now I was paying for it. I had to make it right with my kids, I had to! I was a more humble, patient and driven man now. Now, I felt as if I could survive out there. But was it my time?

Let me tell you, the worst part of hustlin' in prison is the anxiety. You never know when they're coming for you. And you know they are, it's just a matter of when. The jailhouse snitches are yelling your name at the top of their lungs, and you can feel the administration's eyes baring down on you. But you can't stop. To stop only means to give up. Either you keep hustling and vow never to break your positive vibe (for me it was writing) or you suffer early defeat by not even trying. I chose to go against the tide of stagnation and even though I knew my actions were wrong the ends justified the means. I made it all count and somewhat felt better for what I did. Every penny went towards something positive and I never lost sight of the main goal. But just because your intentions are good doesn't mean the deed is. Like the old saying goes: *The road to hell is paved with good intentions...*

I called home two weeks after the check was cut to my attorney and my older brother Eric broke the bad news. "Bro... I'm about to tell you somethin'," he said, "But don't lose it." As soon as he said 'don't lose it' my stomach flipped. Usually when a person tells you not to lose it it's probably because they know you're about to. So I took a deep breath, and braced.

"What is it bruh?" I asked dreading the answer. My second biggest fear was losing someone close to me while in prison.

"Momma had a stroke... She's paralyzed." My ears popped, knees buckled and tears welled in my eyes. "Don't flip out, bruh. She still with us," he coaxed. "Just take it all in and call me back later." Eric knew me better than anybody, so he could practically feel the pain in my chest and stomach, see the tears streaming down my face. He understood the bond my mother and I had, and he knew I was torn.

I hung up the phone hollower than ever that day. Outside of my children my mother and brother were the closest people to my heart. Through thick and thin the three of us always prevailed. We'd gone from the top to the bottom together and remained intact. This was my mother. A person who was and still is my ultimate best friend. To hear her suffering unimaginable pains nearly killed me. And as I sat fully clothed in a bathroom stall—people coming in to urinate and defecate and smoke weed and cigarettes in the stalls beside me—all I could think of was her; the hospital bed, her paralysis, the pain she was enduring. I could've drowned in my tears that day.

The last time I'd cried like that was at my grandmother's funeral in 2003. Before that I can't recall the last time tears soaked my face like that. And I had a lot to clear my head back then: Liquor, weed, and my trusty Xanax. After a few of those, a bottle of this and a couple puffs of that, I was cured. Or at least I felt cured. Now, all I had was a couple grams of bagged up heroin, something I didn't have an urge for.

I'd been drug free for quite some time now. I was back focused, back writing and educating myself, and my second novel, *Omerta*, was near publication. My mind, body and soul was healthy, and then reality hit and suddenly I didn't care about my life anymore. I just wanted away from the pain of knowing my mother was suffering, and heroin was my cure.

I snuck around when I got high, sniffing a little here or a little there, although I really didn't care if people knew. I supported myself and it never interfered with the business aspect of my hustlin'. And thus, sniffin' became a past time, a shelter to hide underneath from all the pain that rained down on me. I dibbed and dabbed for a couple weeks—always after my writing and studying was done—and no one ever knew my secret. My mother turned out okay—she remained paralyzed and her brain kinda slushed—but every thing was back to normal. Or so I thought it was…

*   *   *

January 2012 started out more pleasing than any of my years in prison. I was nearing my 8th full year and my novel had finally hit print. My attorney was optimistic about my appeal and my visits were back on track. My brother had already been to see me that year, as well my old man, aunt, cousin, and grandmother. But I was desperate to see my kids. I craved their touch, yearned to see their smiles for the New Year, and our January 20th visit couldn't get there quick enough!

My son's mother and I maintained a very plutonic relationship over the years. She was a Godsend. Every birthday and every major holiday she brought them to see me. She was a vital piece of their life—and mines for that matter—and whether she knew it or not I thoroughly respected her for her role in our lives. She reminded me of a younger version of my mother. I received pictures on a somewhat regular basis, saw the four of them on visits often, and spoke to them every weekend. She couldn't have been a better mother and friend. But, like always, shit happens.

I spoke to Andrea a couple days before our January 20th visit and everything seemed fine. I called to check up on them and ensure they were making the trip. And surprisingly, Andrea was ecstatic to talk to me. She was never nasty with me when I called but sometimes she could get moody. But I understood. I had left her to assume the role of mother and father of not one child, but three. I understood things could get crazy. But this day she was almost too happy to hear from me. She expressed her gratitude for my acknowledging her and her family in my new book and very subtly expressed how proud she was of me, but I sensed something off in her voice. I couldn't put my finger on it, but it eventually came out. "The cover could've been better," she said referring to my novel, and my acknowledgement was no where near as long as that Ebony girl's, but I guess its cool."

I was hurt. Very hurt. One of the most important and influential people who prompted my change had blatantly put me down. I wanted nothing more than to prove that I wasn't in there pissing away my time, that I was actually going against the tide and trying to improve, but she didn't care. Out of all the years I'd spent writing and reading and educating myself outside the state's discretion and she downed me. I calmly ended the call, changed into my recreation clothes and ran 30 laps around the track collecting myself.

Visiting day had finally come. My hair was freshly tapered, clothes and shoes crispy too, and I smelled great. They called my name over the bullhorn and I walked to the visiting room beaming. The degrading stripdown didn't get to me, nor did the staredown from the C.O's on guard in the visitation room. I couldn't see or think of anything but my babies! I couldn't wait to rub my son's arm and sniff his face (a habit I had since I was a child), and I desperately needed his flesh against mine; to feel his tiny heartbeat against my chest as I hugged him and played in his hair. I literally *needed* those visits.

So, like with every other visiting day, I was greeted by my family with warm hugs and huge smiles. My youngest daughter and son ran up to me as soon as I walked out and Andrea gave me a big hug when I approached their table. Food and beverages marked the spot where each of us sat and it seemed as if everybody were happy to be there. We laughed and joked for a few minutes and my son allowed me to indulge in my habits. Then came the first ripple in the wave pool.

I never speculated jealousy from Andrea. Even after the situation on the phone. I never expected Andrea to be jealous of my success while in prison. She had a man and had long expressed the lack of interest in me. So when she started verbally gnawing at me for all types of random things I was taken aback. She led on a barrage of complaints that revolved around acknowledging other women in my novel (even her own family!) and claimed I hadn't changed a bit. She brought up the fact that I was physically and emotionally abusive to her in the past and that I never cared about her or the kids or I would've never left them behind. She claimed I'd never change, that I'll always be a thug and gangster, and that the new version of me was a fraud. I was dumbfounded. I didn't understand what just happened. I'd long expressed remorse and sorrow for my actions and I'd definitely matured. I was much more respectful, very less likely to respond to a situation by using rage and violence, and sought education and understanding in all ways possible. I made rational decisions (for the most part) and I contributed towards my children's lives immensely. So what was the problem? What was I doing wrong? I didn't know, but I definitely wasn't staying around to find out. I couldn't bring myself to raise my voice or disrespect her. Not anymore. I loved this woman more than I'd ever loved another woman in life and I had already put her through too much. That part of me was gone. So I did the only thing I could at the time: I got up and walked out the visiting room and left them behind. And when I did I was half the man I was when I entered.

<u>Chapter Eight</u>

I once read the only true distance between man and beast is man's vulnerability to emotion. Emotions such as: fear, anger, joy, pride, and sorrow. These are critical elements in nature, elements that can seriously damage man's life. Take for example the situation with my son's mother. Even though she showed sudden ill-will and hatred towards me, I still loved and respected her. I was a fool when I was younger, a fool that thought misogyny and adultery was cool. I'd never loved another woman the way I loved her, but I'd never hurt another woman the way I hurt her either. I was deaf, dumb, and blind before prison, and although I could hear her desperate pleas loud and clear back then, I was too full of myself to right my wrongs. I broke her heart and mistreated her badly and somehow I thought it was love. I'd tear holes in her heart with my cheating and disrespect and somehow thought the lavish gifts I offered her were bandages. I took a young lady who grew up subjected to mental and physical abuse and forced more upon her. And that vulnerability—her vulnerability to prowling figures such as myself—and my weakening vulnerability to the streets, is what connected us. And so, I started feeling like everything I'd done up to that point was useless. If my family and friends didn't acknowledge the change in me then how could I expect the parole board to? They gauge growth by the amount of conduct reports and programs taken by an inmate not by maturation and growth development tests. To be honest, I didn't think they'd ever truly see who I became, and obviously neither would Andrea. My entire walk back to the dormitory from the visit that day I thought of running; running from the torturous pain I felt in my chest, towards the pursuit of my own happiness. For the past eight years I'd made decisions that were predominantly for my loved ones. Sure, I wanted to change, but more than anything I wanted them to see that I was capable of living a life outside of the streets. So I worked steadfastly at strengthening my mind, body, and soul so when the time came I was a impenetrable fortress. But like Augustus Caesar of the Roman era I suffered defeat from within my own empire. Only instead of it being blood leaking from a knife wound it was heroin draining from my nose.

I had relapsed.

*　　　*　　　*

Let me get this straight: Never have I felt like a junkie. Maybe an outcast but never a junkie. I was secluded on a tiny unattached island and didn't wanna be found. I stood despondent, on a small stretch of green canvas and as far as my eyes could see there was nothing but dark water. I was alone, nobody to confide in or share my pain with, only my heartache and imagination, and I was okay with that. The months moved by with a blur and I felt like I was floating on clouds everyday. My second novel (Omerta) was finally complete and I was focusing heavily on advertising and promotion. My debut novel lacked sufficient advertising and promotion but I was sure to break the cycle on my sophomore novel. I had everything planned. I'd hire a graphic designer to design my website and flyers and banners, and secure a couple billboards within the city of Dayton to get my product out there. I had so many plans it was sick, but like always, our plans mean nothing if they're not sanctioned by the Most High God…

A man's heart plans his ways, but the Lord directs his steps.

God had something different up his sleeve for me, and not necessarily good…

*　　　*　　　*

May 2012 an investigation was launched within London Correctional institution targeting heroin on the premises. Not many people within the institution had access to the drug but those who did usually kept it at hand. If a guy wanted to make a little money or get high they knew who to go to. It was that easy. Everyone knew everyone, but so did the authorities, and when they received my name from one of the jail-house snitches they made a follow-up. I was approached and subjected to a full body search, where I was caught red-handed with nearly a gram of uncut heroin. I was mortified. I'd been out-conned, outwitted and outsmarted by a snitch. But who was to blame? I'd gotten beside myself with the drug use and needed to accept full responsibility for my actions—all of them. I needed help, serious help, and while I had this grand plan of prospering in prison and thrusting my books in the spotlight nationally, I'd never considered that the universe might've had something else in store for me? I'd gotten beside myself by supplementing drug use for God's love and I paid for it. I'd created this bogus image in my mind of being stuck on a tiny unattended island when all along *God was the island!* I tried to remove power from the Creator and place things in my own hands and I failed miserably. Now I was back in segregation, and on my way back to Lebanon on a disciplinary hardship. *It can't get any worse*, I thought. *Or can it?*

*   *   *

The ride back to Lebanon was agonizing. Being shackled ankle-to-wrist for eight hours is dreadful, but being shackled ankle-to-wrist for eight hours for wanting to be high is even more upsetting. The usual comings and goings of day-to-day life seem like flashes of hell while you partake them; the cars whizzed by the hot bus like red and white blurs of melted metal and the multitudes of various birds flocked by like colorful smudges of death. I hated it. Sleep came seldom and even if it was possible to get past the gut-wrenching hunger pains and chains and shackles the stifling heat on the bus got to you. This was a physical representation of Prophet John's interpretation of the hereafter in the book of Revelations; this was Hell.

In some strange way I was sort of happy to be back at Lebanon. Reason being, the harsh realities of the land had helped hold me into the man I was. The lifers gave me life and the day-to-day violence made me appreciate the harmonic humdrum of peace while in prison. I mean, how can you not appreciate life and the possibility of freedom when nearly everyone around you has sentences of 30, 40, or 50 years-to-life? Tell me, how can you not gain inspiration from a man that can still sit, stand and smile after being condemned to prison for the remainder of his life? It's impossible. But, I soon found out the times had changed in Lebanon. Most of the old-timers had been weeded out around the same time as I had three years prior, and what few staff members cared back then had disappeared as well. Lebanon was barren now, filled with directionless, ill-advised, wayward youth with no morals, respect, nor appreciation for life. Every thirty minutes there was a "man down" signal indicating a senseless fight throughout the compound, and every eight out of ten people claimed to be a gang member. Their new system of "crashing"—where a person was hit or stabbed by a new recruit on site—had already resulted in countless broken jaws, shattered eye-sockets, missing or broken teeth, and thousands of stitches, and it wasn't gonna stop. If a guy wanted something done to somebody—or just wanted someone out of the way for their own particular reasons—they'd send a minion and the job was done immediately. The minion got their patch (or made their bones) and the man-down signals continued to go off. Everywhere you turned there was blood, teeth and soiled gauze, and the fact that literally anybody could be a target set the entire prison population on edge. Guys walked in packs of ten and twenty, and many of them carried knives or leather fighting gloves in their waistbands. This was definitely not the Lebanon I knew.

It only took ninety days before the violence reached me. It was Halloween 2012 and I was still numb from my denied appeal two weeks prior. I felt like shit on the inside and out but somehow managed to portray my usual jovial self. I was sober, dealing with my issues eternally, and absolutely nothing was gonna throw me off course.

The situation transpired just after evening chow. I was still in the security block for having been transferred from another institution—by way of disciplinary actions—as were the remaining 150 people inside the cellblock. Most were violent offenders and members of the Bloods, Crips, Arian Brotherhood, Gangster Disciples, or the Heartless Felons, and most were potential threats towards the other. They all chanted and whooped and whistled as we filed in from the cafeteria and took our places in front of our cell doors—as they did everyday—and the Correctional Officers stomped down each tier with their black mace guns, shiny batons and menacing faces. Their hostile dispositions were intended to discourage sudden acts of violence like the one about to unfold against an old acquaintance of mine—but it rarely did so. The new breed of inmates in Lebanon were young, wild and heartless.

Unluckily, I was standing next to my old acquaintance when the hit unfolded. We were conversing about old times when a guy maybe 10 years and one-hundred pounds lighter came and blindsided him. The punch was so hard and thunderous that it reverberated through the dayroom and sank in my chest. My acquaintance grabbed his face and buckled over and before I knew it two of the initiator's friends were swarming towards us. I pivoted, looked to my right where a burly teenager was approaching at top speed, and I threw a flurry of punches that connected with his face, neck and chest. The shouts and whoops increased inside the cellblock and within seconds the guards were bearing down on us spraying mace and swinging their batons. Five of us were sprayed, one beat half-conscious with a baton, and we were all thrown in isolation for sentences that ranged from 15 to 45 days. We were all destined for the security block when we were released and most certain to see one another again. A few guys were upset that I had "interfered with their hit" by merely protecting myself and I found myself in the middle of more trouble. I refused to apologize for instinct and therefore ended up fighting my way through a totally different situation. And look how easily that happened. I saw figures in my peripheral and defended myself. I didn't wanna be involved, didn't even know why the hell they were attacking him, but I was still made guilty from association. Talk about a twisted stretch of luck. But I handled my business, cleaned myself up afterwards, and made sure I stayed as far away from my old acquaintance as physically possible…

*   *   *

After being released from the hole for my second rule-19 fight in two years, I was placed in a cell with a person who really tried my patience. Not only was he a snitch and homosexual serial rapist but he was also unhygienic and very disrespectful. His breath and feet shared the same sour stench, he had uncontrollable flatulence and refused to clean up behind himself. He was also mouthy, prying, and as bad as I wanted to feed into his nonsense by punching him I just couldn't. I already had a violent case and a violent record, I couldn't afford another stroke of violence on my record. So my photographs of my children stayed under lock and key and I slept with one eye open. I'd heard stories of parole board inmates getting upwards of ten years for acts of violence while incarcerated and I couldn't afford it. I'd already gotten into two fights and never had a chance to express myself on how the incidents happened, so I suppressed my feelings, constructed my own little world within the cell and focused on my writing. But as soon as I got totally situated a guy appeared at my cell door with some of the most heartbreaking news ever.

We were on the way to the cafeteria for lunch and I had just joined the sea of inmates filing out the main door one-by-one. We looked like cattle being herded to a slop pit, all dressed in blue khakis and blue cotton shirts, all baring the same typical mean-mugs.

When we entered the cafeteria a longtime friend of the family named Andy asked: "You see the news?"

"Nah, why you say that?" I responded and picked up my portion of bland, horribly cooked state rations.

"You might need to call home when we get back. I think somethin' happened with your cousin, Quinton."

"Like what?" I asked skeptically. Quinton was my younger cousin of eight years who was an aspiring rapper and part-time marijuana dealer.

"Somebody got killed."

Quentin? Killin' someone? I thought. *Nah, he ain't that type. Then, again,* I thought, *somebody did shoot him in the process of robbing him two years ago. But since then he's been too focused on his music career to be caught up in any nonsense like that.*

By now we were seated at our table and guys were walking up to me asking questions like, "Hey, was that your people on the news last night? The one who got killed on Gettysburg?"

Killed, on Gettysburg? I looked over at Andy. "Killed?"

His eyes grew wide indicating that the news was new to him too. "I only caught the end. I just seen his picture."

I looked at the other guy. "Killed? Who got killed?" I asked.

"Q. Stone from Residence Park," he answered matter of factly. "I think his mom got shot up too."

My heart dropped. That was my aunt and first cousin he was talking about. This couldn't be. I just spoke to him. Not Quinton. Not the guy who looked up to me even though I was incarcerated. He couldn't be gone. He was too good a man to be shot dead. Sure, he sold a little weed outside of work, but he cared for his mother and sister with all his heart and held a very firm position within the church. This couldn't be true. But it was. I watched the news for myself later on that night and saw what everyone else had seen. Apparently my aunt's boyfriend got violently drunk and beat her. My cousin came home and seen this and immediately pursued his mother's attacker. The end result was Quinton shot dead and my aunt suffering from critical gunshot wounds to the knees and ankles. Her boyfriend was captured hours later and convicted on charges of murder and felonious assault charges and sentenced to thirty years-to-life in prison. People ask me all the time if I feel my situation and the situation with Quinton parallels in terms of grief and sorrow, and while I feel they're totally different in sense and nature I still feel the pain that underlines them both in the pit of my chest. And to that I say, Rest In Peace William Evans and Quinton Stone, may your souls be with the angels…

PART III:
THE REFINEMENT

<u>Chapter Nine</u>

Like every other New Years Eve, I brought the year 2013 in in prayer. So while the other inmates of Cell Block K were screaming, chanting, and pounding on their cell doors as a show of appreciation for having braved another year of Lebanon, I was perched on top of my bunk, eyes closed, palms pressed together in an arch under my chin, as I strived to become closer to the presence of God within me.

Dear heavenly Father, please forgive me for my sins... The sins I know I've done, the sins I don't know I've done, and the sins I'll commit in the future for I'm only a mere human being... Watch over my family and friends Father, by keeping them safe, secure, healthy and out of harms way, and please grant me the strength and wits to grow beyond my environment.... I know there's not a lot of room for growth here in Lebanon, Father, but please allow me to prosper in all ways possible... I concluded with a few brief words for Quinton, Tweet and my late grandmother, and closed my eyes happy to have made it through another year in Lebanon myself.

But while I was embarking on a new year within my journey in the wilderness, several of my closest friends were nearing the lonely road of incarceration row themselves. Within twelve months I witnessed seven of my childhood friends sentenced to more than a hundred and twenty years in federal and state prisons combined. I witnessed devoted fathers snatched violently from the arms of their children, good men torn from the minds and hearts of the women who loved them most. And these were decent guys I'm talking about. Guys who—albeit a life of crime— took damned good care of those they loved. They accepted collect calls from dozens of prisoners monthly, put money on our telephone and commissary accounts, even took time out of their lives to visit us and bring gifts to our children around holidays and birthdays. They were decent men to some degree, caught in the same snare I'd been caught in when I was thirteen, chasing an object that didn't wanna be caught, objectifying a game that was more of a consequence than anything. They had fallen just as I had fallen so many years ago. The only difference was they left a lot more behind. Sure, some of them sold drugs and broke the law, but they were only playing the hands life dealt them.

It's amazing how the streets fool us hustlers into thinking we can win. When in all actuality we have a better shot at winning big in Vegas than succeeding in the streets. Take for example my guys. A couple were near millionaires and the others weren't far behind. They lived good and played better, but in they end received the same fate as a guy like myself—decades of years in prison—their sentences to be executed immediately. No two-hundred for passing go, no hug from Mama or kiss from the babies, off to prison to serve hard time with the rest of the losers. Their money, cars, and jewelry misappropriated by untrustworthy friends and family, all of their hard work taken in vain. It killed me to watch this happen, to sit back and watch the process unfold. *Something has to change*, I told myself. *Something definitely has to change.* But what I had to understand is that before I could love vertically I had to learn how to love horizontally. Which meant I had to start with my own spirit and work upward before I focused on healing the others around me. So that's exactly what I did! I began ordering self-help books and books on spiritual guidance and I worked steadfastly at broadening my writing skills. I started reading and writing poetry as well as non-fiction and my skill set developed. I told myself if I was gonna reach the masses that books like *From Soldier To King* and *Escaping the Prison Within* were the proper tools to do so. So I wrote and wrote and wrote and suddenly the pages blossomed from my notebook like crimson roses from the concrete. Before I knew it not only had I penned my third fiction novel (titled *Everybody Dies But Not Everybody Lives)* and laid the ground work for both *From Soldier To King* and *Escaping the Prison Within,* but I joined forces with my old organization 7th Step and was immediately offered a seat on the board as Vice President. I started a self-help class inside the prison called *What's Your Issue?* and the class was an instant success! I had guys all over the compound signing up for my class, even state-funded administrative facilitators sitting in to take notes. To know not only how the itty-bitty inmate before them charmed the roomful of lions, tigers and bears, but more importantly how he *taught* them. They sat in awe as reputed gangsters, hustlers, and murderers practically begged to share their issues with the class. They were eager to learn, speak, and be heard; to be felt, understood, and led in a new direction in life. They felt enlightened, appreciated, and positive for a change. And although it was a beautiful thing while it lasted, sadly *What's Your Issue?* only lasted one tenure. The administration shut us down soon after citing that we housed "too many gang members" and "predominantly problematic inmates." *WTF?!* I thought. *But aren't those the ones who need help? Aren't those the inmates we should target?*

Then a conversation I had with an old case manager a year ago came back to me. We were discussing programming and advancement at other prisons versus no programming at Lebanon and he told me plain as plaid: "Places like Lebanon aren't designed for you to win Mr. Stone... They're designed for you to lose!"

*   *   *

The prison system was a Catch-22 for guys like me. With virtually no programming available until you've reached the 5 year mark of your sentence it's difficult to establish a good institutional record for a judicial release or parole board hearing. By then you've scored so lowly on the "risk assessment score" that your chances are slim next to none of productive advancement beyond that point. During the risk test you're asked a series of questions such as date of birth, date of last felony committed, last grade completed , and Estimated Date of Terminated Sentence, and after all this is infractioned in you're given a score. Your score to my understanding determines if you're "bumped up" or "bumped down" on the waiting list for programs such as drug and alcohol, behavioral classes, or educational. These are essentially the same programs that an inmate must have when not only expecting a positive outcome but also with their futures. Our lives depend on these years. But when you're not an at risk prisoner you get the back of the bus. I wasn't violent, didn't get excessive tickets, I had my G.E.D., hadn't caught a violent felony in over 10 years, and my EDS was more than 5 years away. I qualified lowly on the risk assessment score but my life wasn't over. I read over two hundred books in the first ten years of my incarceration and I amassed more than one-thousand hours of studying. I helped hundreds of people further themselves in life through classes like 7ᵗʰ Step and *What's Your Issue?* and mentored dozens of others. Yes it's true I got hooked on heroin, had a couple of fights and was found with drugs on my person and sentenced to seven extra months for it, but with the entire weight of the world on my shoulders I prevailed. But, that doesn't mean suicide as a way out didn't cross my mind…

*   *   *

Some days, suicide seemed like a valid escape from the repetition of prison. You lay around wallowing in depression and pity and you secretly wish and pray for the reaper to come and claim your life. You feel so alone that the unknown becomes a better option. You play the options of death around in your mind and consider the easiest way out. You contemplate—maybe even situate—then ask yourself about family. *Will they care? Will they miss me when I'm gone? Will they even come to view my body at my funeral?* You ask yourself all these things and a decision is made. You either decide that your life is too tiring and burdenous and you give up, or you gain strength from somewhere and you choose life. I kept my children at the forefront of my mind, telling myself over and over that they loved me and needed me and wanted me no matter what. The suicidal thoughts subsided and I slowly weaved myself back into the life I loved to hate. I laughed, I cried, but I remained alive. I saw twenty people die in prison over the course of ten years and fourteen of them were victims of suicide. One minute they were full of life and the next minute they were gone. And I don't know if I consider them cowards or not, but I will say this: The walls of prison are lonely but the walls of Hell are even lonelier...

*　　　*　　　*

One of the worst things I saw while incarcerated were guys being released from serving long prison sentences only to re-succumb to the streets immediately after. Because not only had I been this person before (to some degree) but I now knew what it felt like to be skipped over. I used to sit and watch from my prison window as hundreds—thousands—of ex-cons were released back out into the world and I longed for a place in their shoes. I pictured myself being dressed out in their places, greeting their wonderful families as if they were mines, even counting their meager gate pay with plans of spending every penny of it on things productive. I wanted what these people had so badly that if given the opportunity I'd probably take it. But I couldn't. Their fate was theirs and my fate was mine. All I could do from that point was sit back and watch as they left, hoping, praying, that they got out there and succeeded.

I did time with two individuals who got out and failed miserably: Damian Wesley and Harvey Jones. I met Wesley when I transferred to London Correctional in 2009 and Harvey Jones I'd known pretty much all my life. Both were good people on the surface, but both suffered from serious psychological issues that were left untreated. Wesley served fifteen-years-to-life for allegedly murdering his best friend and roommate over a woman, and Jones served ten years for the alleged rape and assault of his girlfriend and suspected child's mother. Both paid their debts to society and both were released from prison with reliable skill sets and stable jobs awaiting them. Wesley used his certificate in paralegals assistance to secure a job at a highly esteemed law firm in the city of Dayton, Ohio, while Jones held a firm position at a local barbershop making good money. Both men were doing great in the beginning of their release but within a year were back in jail awaiting charges of capital murder. Wesley confessed to shooting his girlfriend and murdering her teenage daughter out of jealousy, and Jones allegedly murdered his ex-girlfriend in front of her infant son. Wesley died in the Montgomery County Jail while awaiting trial, and as of this writing, Jones' case hadn't been resolved.

But let's not reflect on the *what*, rather the *how?* Both of these men had suppressed issues of rage and jealousy and both were released back out into society without treatment. Jones served ten years for violently beating and raping someone before jumping off a bridge in an effort to commit suicide, and Wesley was said to have put his best friend and roommate in the headlock before fatally shooting him. They both became productive members of society and both were doing extremely good on the surface, but underneath they were ticking time-bombs ready to explode. Neither of these individuals were treated for their issues (to my knowledge) but it's obvious they needed it. Countless lives were damaged in the process of these generational curses perpetuated and the sad part was the problem still existed. People like Wesley and Jones need treatment throughout their entire tenures of incarceration, not just the last few months or years of their prison stays. By waiting to address their issues didn't necessarily mean they were cured, it only meant the issues were lying dormant and had become somewhat controllable. In this case the inmates continued to suffer mentally and psychologically and society and the tax-payers financially. The prisons remained jammed-packed and the recidivism rate continued to rise. We needed a serious change, but would we ever get it was the question.

<u>Chapter Ten</u>

The year 2014 turned out to be even more rewarding than I anticipated. Well, at first. I met a beautifully spirited woman who seemed to genuinely care for me, launched my website *pimpinthepen.com*, published my second novel (titled Omerta), and managed to finish writing my third (Everybody Dies But Not Everybody Lives). I secured the role as editor-in-chief at Educated Thugs Publications and picked up several sponsors who funded promotional items such as flyers, posters, and banners for my books and website. They created E-flyers and YouTube commercials and blasted them over social media while a nationally known and well-respected research team picked apart my case for further appellate issues. My lady friend and I were growing closer as the days tumbled by and my upcoming security review was growing in the distance. I was dying to be shipped back out to another less problematic and stress-filled environment, and as of then I qualified. I hadn't had a ticket since the 2012 Halloween fight incident and I honestly felt like things were looking up for me. I was ten years in on my now 15 and a half year sentence (I received seven extra months for possession of heroin charge in London Correctional) and finally—finally!—I was able to start setting a positive example on paper for the parole board. I'd taken a long inward approach at re-cultivating my mind and behavior and felt I'd succeeded. I published two novels, launched a website, successfully completed and facilitated several programs within the prison, written fundraising proposals for non-profit organizations, helped raise thousands of dollars for charities such as Toys for Tots and the Lebanon City Schools District, encouraged hundreds of wayward youth while editing manuscripts for my publisher and several of our authors. But like always, the actions of my past came back to haunt me…

This time it was my immediate past that came back to bite me. My days of wheeling and dealing in London Correctional had been made aware to the investigator at Lebanon and I was under watch. My mail and telephone calls were monitored and they paid close attention to every move I made on visits. I was suspected of living up to my old ways in Lebanon and the investigator there leaned on me hard. His theory was that I was actively involved with drugs due to my associates and he wanted to use me to catch them in his snare. So he detained me one afternoon and threatened to write a conduct report against me if I didn't further his investigation. I was marked as a drug dealer and addict from London Correctional but never a snitch. I grew up in the era where you minded your business and took your charge if the situation occurred. So when the inquiries came regarding the dealings of my childhood friends I very calmly denied any involvement. And I was being honest! I hadn't touched or even seen any drugs or tobacco since May of 2012 and didn't have any urge to. But he was infuriated and lashed out with vengeance. He locked me up and wrote a ticket stating that I: *Dealt, conducted, facilitated, or participated in a transaction, occurring in whole or in part, within a institution, or involving any inmate, staff member or another for which payment of any kind is made, promised, or expected.* In my case the dealing came from the sale of a pair of designer Cartier glasses, Air Force gym shoes and commissary fifty cents on the dollar. My youngest daughter's fourteenth birthday was approaching fast and I had promised her a few things. Problem was, technically I was dealing and my actions were punishable by months in segregation, restrictions such as phone, electronics and visitation, and increased points on my upcoming security level hearing. It was bad, very bad. But the worst part was, I was set up!

The money I received to purchase birthday gifts for my daughter came in the form of prepaid credit card refills called Moneypaks, which were very common amongst inmates. How the system worked was one inmate would provide another inmate with a refill pack and that inmate would in turn provide their family member on the outside the number to load onto their credit cards. The transaction is totally legal amongst people on the outside but on the inside it violates prison policy. So while I was doing a good deed by taking the shoes off my feet and food out my mouth to ensure that my daughter was somewhat content for her birthday I was breaking rules. *No dealing or sharing whatsoever.* But to the investigator I was a pawn. He thought I knew things and his conduct report was leverage. If I didn't offer substantial assistance "I was done," he said to me. But I couldn't help him. Not only did I not have a single clue as to what these guys were up to, but I wouldn't tell him if I did. Hell, I didn't even know the pre-paid credit card thing was under scrutiny. Sure, I wanted to put a smile on my baby's face but I'm absolutely positive had she known the risk involved she would've held out. And how was I to know the investigator was conducting an active investigation against the use of pre-paid credit card refills if I wasn't doing anything? He claimed amongst the twenty numbers he recovered throughout the institution that three of them led to me. These numbers were said to have been subpoenaed by the Department Of Corrections Operation Support System and traced back to my family. I was done, as he said, but all he wanted my homeboys. He knew I was out of the game—even confessed this to me during his recorded interview—but was so adamant about catching these guys that he decided to send a message through me. *This is my castle, my jungle, and I do what I want... Give up whatever you're doing or you'll end up like Mr. Stone.* And it was clear that he could definitely do whatever he wanted. These guys knew first hand that I had changed. I rarely spent time with them anymore and I sure as hell didn't use or sell drugs or tobacco. I bought the bare necessities from commissary and read and wrote all day.

How was I still dealing? I even offered to take a urine and a lie detector test. But he wanted my associates and that was that. I refused to speak with him any longer and was immediately confined to an isolation cell.

My infringements against D.R.C. Policies not only got me thrown me in the hole for sixty days but it also killed my shot at transferring and painting a positive picture for the members of the parole board. The investigator deceptively placed the total sum of monies ever added to my families three pre-paid credit cards—which came close to $12,250 over the course of six months—and alleged that my actions within the institution accounted for this. But I didn't have a red cent to my name. The money I received for my daughter's birthday had long been gone and my inmate account said something like $7.00. I sure as hell didn't have twelve-thousand dollars. I appealed the decision stating the fact that my family used their cards for day-to-day things such as gas, food, shopping, bills and utilities and that the investigators actions were deceitful in applying the overall sum on my ticket to strengthen his claims of guilt, but they denied stating the charge of dealing was proven and the amount wasn't necessary. They shut my family's credit cards down due to suspicious activity and it created even more distance between us.

The silver lining in the whole situation was I learned more about Self and God. I learned no matter how bad I wanted something to happen—nor how hard I tried—that unless it was sanctioned by the most High God it wouldn't happen. *Man may make many plans in his life but the Lord will direct his path.* I needed to learn how to listen to God instead of trying to get God to listen to me. I needed to learn no matter how hard I plotted, planned and strategized on freeing myself that if it wasn't a part of God's plan for me that my endeavors wouldn't bear fruit. I had mistakenly figured since He'd rescued me from the blazing fire of the streets so many times—removing me from crumpled automobiles, violent gun battles and situations where individuals were aiming to take my life, unscathed—that somehow he'd given me the discretion to take my life where I wanted it to go. But He hadn't, and had this situation not occurred—unfortunate as it was—I would've never developed into the man I had. I would've never came to know Self and God the way I did, never tapped into the presence of peace within me, nor would I have ever sought the craft of writing. I was more patient, humble, understanding and frugal in life. I learned to seek knowledge and understanding in all that I did and to never fret over things uncontrollable. I learned the laws of Build and Destroy—build a new life and new ways of living while destroying all old evils—and the fact that there is undoubtedly a molecular balance in life—the yin and yang. I learned that too much of anything is not good for you, that you reap what you sow, and that karma is always ever-present in our lives. It took a lot to get to where I was I but could honestly say it was all worth it.

I never asked to be placed in the unfortunate situation I was in that night, and if permitted I would surely breathe life back into William Evans, Sr. He was very unrelenting in his actions but we are all men and all flawed to some degree. My heart and soul goes out to his children and as long as I'm willing and able I'll continue to pray for them. And although I didn't truly understand the dynamics of my plea agreement back then I can say I made the best of my sentence. I took my curse of condemnation and used it as a blessing. I re-cultivated and re-calibrated my mind so that it was peace and prosperity at the forefront of it instead of drugs, violence, and fornication. I learned who I was as an individual and fell in love with this person. I entered the flaming bowels of hell a lowly soldier and emerged a king.

Freedom is an element of man's heart and soul, not of his physicality... You can incarcerate his body but never his mind... He lives, he grows, he loves and he shows... ***For man is King and the world is his throne.***

MEMOIRS OF A POETIC PRISONER

Parts I, II (Non-Fiction)

"Poetry Done Right"

Q. Dillard

"This collection of poems shows the depth and range of a prisoner..."

W. Tims

"Spoken word in written form"

L. Wright

"Deep!"

Z. Givens

"Comparable To Tupac's Concrete Rose."

R. Williams

Educated Thug Publications

Synopsis

From Soldier To King is a compelling memoir that delves into the life of Ohio prisoner and self-proclaimed "cell-entrepreneur" Jamarr Rodney Stone, Sr., who wrote and co-wrote novels such as *Everybody Dies But Not Everybody Lives, TrapStarz, Omerta,* and *Pound For Pound* (All written under the pseudonym Hector Tha Plug). Jamarr gives his readers a transparent and in-depth look at his journey of maturation from a lowly-ranked soldier in a war of self-perpetuated crime and stupidity, onto regal king in a world where accountability and understanding lead to spiritual richness and financial success.

"In this gripping tale of fear, abandonment, drug abuse and contemplated suicide [Jamarr] touches the bottom of every soul."

Shawn G. Lillard, Re-Entry Activist and Founder Of Thoroughbred Fitness

"After one night of fun led to a sentence of life imprisonment, Jamarr found himself back in the bowels of life's underworld, and managed to triumph!"

Mr. B. Barron Hawkings, Re-Entry Activist

****

"His brutal honesty and unfathomable candor shows utter appreciation for every bump and bruise his soul suffered through life…"

Shirley McCartney of Prison Legal Discovery

****

Jamarr Rodney Stone, Sr., a proud father of 3 became the voice of prisoners and ex-cons while serving time in the Ohio penal system. Not one to bend, break or fold easily, Jamarr took the pain and anguish embedded in his environment and used it to mine a diamond.

Now an advocate for re-entry and reducing the recidivism rate in prisons and jails across the globe, Jamarr uses his depictions of the streets and street life to better his community. With only a few years left on his mandatory sentence he plans to reach, teach, and enlighten the masses through his literature.

Educated Thug Publications

Made in United States
Troutdale, OR
12/11/2024

26295248R00066